Data An

Practical Data Analysis and Statistical Guide to Transform and Evolve Any Business

Leveraging the Power of Data Analytics, Data Science, and Predictive Analytics for Beginners

By: Isaac D. Cody

DATA ANALYTICS

PRACTICAL DATA ANALYSIS AND STATISTICAL GUIDE TO TRANSFORM AND EVOLVE ANY BUSINESS

Leveraging the power of Data
Analytics, Data Science, and
Predictive Analytics for Beginners

ISAAC D. CODY

Preview of this book

Have you ever wanted to use data analytics to support your business?

With many businesses, data analytics can just that plus more. It's a great system to see how things are going, and you can collect the information to form conclusions through this. But how does it work? What are the nuances of this? Well, that's where this book comes in.

In this book, you'll learn the following:

- What are data analytics

- The importance of big data

- How to conduct data analytics

- Why a business needs this for success and prosperity now, and in the future

With data analytics, you can save your business, and this book will further prove to you the importance of this subject, what it can do for you, and how you can use data analytics to make your business shine and grow

Table of Contents

Introduction

Chapter 1   The Importance of Data Analytics and Why Your Business Should Use It

Chapter 2   How to Handle Big Data

Big Data and Its Issues

Grabbing and Grasping Big Data

Utilizing Big Data for Business

Chapter 3   The Benefits and Challenges of Data Management

Keys to Effective Data Management

Chapter 4   Real World Examples of Data Management

An Example of Ineffectual Usage

An Example of Effectual Usage

Chapter 5   The Different Types of Data Analytics

Four Kinds of Big Data Business Intelligence

Chapter 6   They all Work Together: Data Management, Data Mining, Data Integration and Data Warehousing

Chapter 7   Conducting Data Analysis for Your Business

A Step by Step Guide

Chapter 8   An Organizational Approach to Data Analytics

Chapter 9   Data Visualization

Chapter 10   Using Social Media

Social Media Analytics

Tools to Help Manage Social Media

Social Media Strategies for the Business Owner

Chapter 11   How Data Analytics Can Sustain any Business

How You Can Collect Data for Analysis Today

Conclusion

Introduction

I want to thank you and congratulate you for downloading the book

Data Analytics: Practical Data Analysis and Statistical Guide to Transform and Evolve Any Business, Leveraging the power of Data Analytics, Data Science, and Predictive Analytics for Beginners

This book contains proven steps and strategies on how to become proficient with big data, data analysis, and predictive analytics, even if you have never studied statistical science. This book takes you from the beginning concepts of data analytics to processing the information, structuring your organization, and even security issues with data management. From the knowledge contained within this book the business owner can create and install big data analytics in even the smallest business.

Data analysis has been proven to change the business world. Companies that are using data analysis for their business decisions are moving ahead of the competition by leaps and bounds. Armed with the knowledge supplied from their analysts, business owners and organizations are making better business decisions regarding marketing, sales and forecasting, to name just a few helpful functions of data analysis.

Here's an inescapable fact: you will need data analysis to keep up with the competition, because they are using it now, in real-time, to make their business decisions.

If you do not develop your understanding of data analysis and big data, you will be left behind in the dust. Your sales may drop and your business may be in jeopardy as a result of inexperience and the lack of information about a growing and necessary trend in business intelligence.

This book is an amazing resource that defines data analysis and the tools and methods that make it successful.

Good luck!

Chapter 1 The Importance of Data Analytics and Why Your Business Should Use It

Data analytics is the buzzword of the decade. Everyone is discussing and promoting data analytics from healthcare to big business. Small business and mega-corporations are touting the advantages of using Big Data to transform their business practices. Warehouses, trucking companies and suppliers are raving about the money they have saved using Data Mining to overhaul their organizations. Is it hype or is it the new Casino, offering cash at every pull of the slot machine handle (or in this case, the data set)?

Data analytics (DA) is the process of interpreting raw data for the purpose of informing the individual (or group) the conclusions derived from the data. Data analytics are used throughout industry to make business decisions on inventory, cash-flow, sales projections, customer characteristics, and loss-prevention strategies, just to name only a few of the practical uses. In science, data analytics are used to prove and disprove theories.

The concept of business analytics and big data has been around since the 1950s to predict insights and trends in the consumer markets. The difference between data collection sixty years ago and today is that today's information set is almost in real time. Today businesses can receive the information in thirty minutes or less to make an immediate business decision. This gives companies that use data analysis a big competitive edge over a company that does not.

The data that is received today by a corporate executive is thorough, fast and reliable. This allows the decision maker to determine the best course of action within minutes of receiving the desired information, rather than weeks, months or even years as previously experienced.

Businesses are tapping into the data mines to utilize the information in many ways, including, but not limited to:

1.	**Cost reduction for data storage**. In 1981 it cost $700,000 to store 1GB of information. In 1996 that cost was $295.00 and in 2014 that same storage cost was only $00.03. (*source:* http://www.mkomo.com/cost-per-gigabyte-update)

2.	**Opportunity for real data for R&D**. Customers are now very vocal about their wants and needs. A new product launch on Twitter can determine quickly the interest in an innovative product design. Data analysis allows immediate feedback for research and development of market trends.

3.   **Inventory and product analysis.** Using data analysis, a company can see what is popular on the shelves and what products need dusting off and moved on out of the store and off the valuable shelf space. Why do grocers' place the most utilized products on the very top and very bottom shelves? They know those products will always sell but the products with the highest markup are at eye-level for the consumer.

Lenovo was designing a new keyboard for their customers, but failed to recognize their loyal customer base in the gaming industry. After using data analytics, Lenovo changed their design to incorporate the gamers' needs and launched a worthy product that brought millions in sales. Data analytics saved their product and increased their profits.

Data analytics is by no means limited to the retail sector. Other businesses use data analytics to increase their profitability and efficiency. Here are a few uses that are currently being adopted by industries:

Travel and Hospitality

Customer satisfaction is very hard to measure but the key to a thriving enterprise. Big data analytics give the management instant access to customer preferences as they check-in, at customer decision points, and even as they leave the facility. This gives management the opportunity to rectify grievances as they occur, turning a potential customer relations bomb into a satisfactory experience for all parties concerned.

Health Care

In the health care industry, big data is changing the way records are kept, research is analyzed, and patient care is managed. The result is a better method of caring for the patient with a computerized record that can follow the patient no matter treatment is given. In addition, sometimes a new procedure or medicine is available immediately because of the instantaneous information of a query. Staffing for hospitals has been transformed also with data analysis, allowing the care facilities to schedule more personnel in the peak times and less for the slower times.

Government

Local police forces are using data analytics to determine the areas with the greatest crime statistics, where more foot patrols would be advantageous, and even the peak times for burglaries and petty crimes. The technology of analysis can pinpoint the problem areas in a suburb or city without sacrificing the limited manpower for surveillance.

Small and mid-size businesses have the same opportunities for collecting data as large factions, but it will be helpful to keep in mind these strategies:

To tap into the mainstream of consumers there must be a digital presence for the business. Customers and clients that are shopping for services and products go to websites and Social Media for opinions, reports, comparisons and reviews.

The website should be straightforward and honest. It should also describe the benefits of the product or service without exaggeration or misrepresentation. Consumers know hype when they see it, and will studiously avoid those websites as potential outlets of information or products. The website should be enabled to give information and to collect information.

Website analytics will gather the demographics of the customer, their interests, their entry point, their boredom and "click off" point, and their favorite social media sites.

If the website is designed correctly with many points of interaction, the client or customer will specify their needs and wants before they realize they have been "mined".

Small Business Example

Here is a good example of a small business that used big data:

A local bakery finds the chocolate chip cookie sales are booming, with orders by the dozen on both the website and from call-in orders. The chocolate cupcakes, however, become slower and slower to move. The baker reads the remarks on the website and finds this innocuous remark: "I love the chocolate cupcakes and the chocolate chip cookies, but I can buy 12 chocolate chip cookies for the price of only 2 cupcakes."

This data became an "aha" moment for the baker. The baker quickly made a separate page for just cookie sales (to continue the chocolate chip cookie trend), but also changes the product offering of full-sized cupcakes to mini-cupcakes. Four mini-cupcakes were priced the same as the chocolate chip cookies by the dozen. The baker also placed a coupon special on the Facebook listing of "buy one dozen assorted cookies and receive a free mini-cupcake of your choice, by mentioning this ad." Sales of all cookies and the new product increased.

Chapter 2   How to Handle Big Data

Big Data and Its Issues

Big data is the data mined that is too large, disorganized or unstructured for an analysis using the traditional technology and techniques currently used in data management. The quantity of data is less important than the how the data is used and categorized.

Big data is divided by three sectors: volume, velocity and variety. Companies are inundated with huge amounts of data and need ways to identify and utilize the data sets.

Regardless of the management issues, big data is still very valuable for a business or organization. Big data makes information transparent and usable. Now that organizations are collecting larger amounts of data, it is much less expensive to store in digital formatting than it ever was by tape. Management uses performance data to explore trends in sick days and employee tardiness, product inventory, movement, and even storage capacity. Other businesses are using data to explore forecasting for budgets and purchasing decisions.

Big data aids companies in segmenting their customer base so that they can tailor the product offerings to the customer needs and desires. More importantly, big data is being utilized in Research and

Development to improve the next generation of service and product offerings.

Grabbing and Grasping Big Data

Companies now have to use new storage, computing, collecting, analysis and techniques to capture and crunch the big data. Even though the technology challenges and even the priorities of individual firms are different, they all have the same issues: older computer systems, incompatible formats, and incomplete integration of data that inhibits the interpretation of the database information.

There are new approaches available for crunching the data to assist with quality management of big data. The best approach will analyze the volume, variety and complexity of the data before making purchasing decisions.

Big data has open source technologies for the database management systems, including Hadoop and Cassandra. There are also several business intelligence software products on the market that report, present and analyze the finished product to the business owner.

Utilizing Big Data for Business

It is estimated that businesses only use 5 percent of the information they receive. This leaves a big space for improvement, which may be filled with the technological stack of implements needed for Big data analysis. There is a requirement of storage, computing, visualization software and analytical software, to start the list. There will the need for additional personnel and probably an IT department.

Does investing in big data payoff in the ROI? In a nutshell, positively. The McKinsey Global Institute anticipates that a business that correctly utilizes big data could increase the operating margin by over 60 percent, a huge sum.

Here are the steps suggested to implement big data in your organization:

- Inventory all data related assets

- Move the management to embrace a data-driven worldview

- Develop technology implementation

- Address policy issues including data security, privacy and property

- Identify opportunities and risks

Data security is of particular importance. Databases contain confidential information that may be trade secrets, personal medical information, and even copyrighted materials. Data should be centralized and secure. Encryption is not an option due to the large amounts of data and the time and personnel that would be required to continue such a practice. Protection of the database begins with the first step mentioned, inventory all sources of input. Only when the scope of the contributing sources is analyzed can businesses determine which security measures need revamping and which particular products with take care of the job.

Chapter 3   The Benefits and Challenges of Data Management

Long ago and far away the business owner would look at a new product, listen to the sales presentation from the jobber, and decide upon whether to purchase the product based on their "gut" intuition. Just like the general store with a post office and gas station, those days are gone.

This is the age of information. Businesses must keep current with trends, market dynamics, consumer preferences, and economic pressures to make the appropriate decisions regarding their presence in the marketplace. The enormous amount of information that is available requires educated persons that are comfortable and accurate in interpreting the data provided.

Case Western Reserve University in Cleveland has recently announced there will soon be a shortage of 190,000 analytics personnel and over 1.5 million data managers. This problem will mostly affect the small and medium sized businesses that cannot afford to hire a personal data analyst on a shoestring budget.

The demand for Information Technology Project Managers with big data skills increased by 123.6% last year, and big data skilled Computer Systems Analysts increased 89.8%, according to Forbes Magazine.

(source: http://www.forbes.com/sites/louiscolumbus/2014/12/29/where-big-data-jobs-will-be-in-2015/#2caeda00404a)

Even when a business has access to data analytics there are still challenges for the business besides how to use the information provided. One of these challenges is Data Management.

Data management is the organizational management of the data and gathered information for security, limited access, and storage issues. Tasks that the data management requires include governance policies, database management systems, integration of data systems, data security, source identification, segregation of data and storage issues.

Keys to Effective Data Management

Data management issues are not a new dilemma. As long as data has been collected the businesses have been dealing with the problematic issue of keeping data pristine. Now, with the increase in data and marketing automation, data security has moved to the pinnacle of the problem areas.

If data isn't clean or relevant, it is of no use to the marketing and business primary officers. Data management requires constant surveillance as hackers are waiting to scoop up and destroy millions of relevant information and resources. There are few things that should be automatic for security issues with data, such as:

1.   **Limit Access**

Many times the access to materials and information is wide open to all employees to modify. Office managers, sales personnel, and office staff should not have the ability to enter the database and change, access or delete and add information. The best way to control this situation is to establish boundaries, or limited access.

Set controls based on specific functions, such as marketing personnel are limited to viewing market data, but not to editing. Determine which person in the organization will do all the data changes including additions/deletions and actions (such as changing contact information for the client). Establish data import and export rules so that secured data is not flying out the door and so that viruses are not being uploaded. Create a master list of data so that information is neither duplicated nor compromised.

2.   **Create a Data Map**

A data map is a flow chart data the route of data, delineating the intake and output, the departmental integration, and the use for each data entry. Data mapping is an ongoing exercise that maintains controls and data consistency.

3.   Organize your Data in Segments

Data is not about quantity but instead about quality. It does no good to have millions of names in the database if your clientele is in the hundreds. It is not helpful to have hundreds of names in the database if you have no organization for retrieval.

Instead, separate the data by your needs. Examples could be by sex, age, address demographics, zip code, contact preferences, etc. Correctly segmenting the database can make the data come alive with potential whereas a disordered database will look and feel like chaos.

Begin with your current active customer base. Segment them into demographics and then by purchasing habits. Connect with your customers on a regular basis to glean their input on your products and services.

4.   **Data Hygiene**

Data hygiene is the process of keeping data clean and current. Old data and corrupted data will only clutter your database and possibly even infect all of your records. Just like the previous functions, hygiene should be provided on a regular basis to ensure the data is not decayed or contaminated.

The importance of maintaining a pristine and organized database cannot not be overlooked. If the data isn't good, all the contacts and marketing projects will not succeed if they are addressed to the wrong contact point. To enhance the value of your database for marketing and sales endeavors, do not neglect database management.

Chapter 4   Real World Examples of Data Management

An Example of Ineffectual Usage

- John Belushi, 33
- Chris Farley, 33
- Jimi Hendrix, 27
- Philip Seymour Hoffman, 46
- Whitney Houston, 48
- Michael Jackson, 50
- Janis Joplin, 27
- Heath Ledger, 28
- Cory Monteith, 31
- River Phoenix, 23
- Elvis Presley, 42
- Prince, aged 57
- Anna Nicole Smith, 39
- Amy Winehouse, 27

These celebrities have a sad connection: They all died from a drug overdose at a too young age.

The prescription drug-monitoring program can inform prescribers (doctors and nurse practitioners) and dispensers (pharmacists) to establish controls for drug abuse and diversion of opioids, the major contributor to the aforementioned deaths. Celebrities only make up a small percentage of the yearly deaths attributed to drug overdoses. The US Centers for Disease Control and Prevention (the CDC) has established that it is the primary cause of accidental death in the United States. At the last published data analysis, it was determined there were over 47,000 drug overdoses in 2014. Prescription pain killers were responsible for 18,893 of those deaths.

The names of these drugs are common prescriptions when one has surgery or a broken arm or just about any circumstance that requires a trip to the local hospital emergency room: Percocet, Lortab, OxyContin, Fentanyl, Vicodin, Morphine and Xanax are just a few examples. Xanax is a benzodiazepine, not a painkiller, but is lethal when ingested with an opioid, even at the minimal quantity of just one dose.

For preventing this epidemic of drug overdose, the separate states have established databases to monitor prescriptions of the products. This database entails the dosage, the frequency the prescription is filled, and the prescribing doctor, in order to determine which patients may be diverting or mismanaging their dosages and which patients are frequenting different doctors and hospitals within a thirty-day period to acquire more drugs.

The concept is great: Have one database that combines the data from various and multiple sources of pharmacies and medical personnel to combat the issue. Unfortunately, the database has several problems that prevent effective management.

- Data is derived from multiple sources and is time-consuming and complex.

- The data is incomplete as many physicians don't take the time to consult the database. Although the installation of the system is mandatory in 49 states, only 22 states require compliance, and no one is monitored for conformity.

- There are too few personnel to conduct real-time analysis of the information. It is fed into the database but not retrieved effectively.

Leading Data Analytics at SAS Institute have addressed the issue in the report *Data and Analytics to Combat the Opioid Epidemic.* Their take is that the information at present is almost unusable.

Source: http://www.sas.com/en_us/whitepapers/iia-data-analytics-combat-opioid-epidemic-108369.html

With better analytics and interpretation physicians could develop improved treatment protocols, patient education and policy boundaries. For example:

- Physicians can compare their treatments with their peers to determine specific patterns of early drug addiction.

- Insurance and government payment systems can catalog the potential misuse or diversion, avoiding the expense costs of paying for fraud.

- Larger hospital and public health systems could develop better educational programs, treatment protocols and resource decisions.

- Pharmacies could compare their dispensing data to determine geographic overlap in abuse, among other factors.

- States could utilize the database for funding treatment centers by demographical information.

Combining and segmenting the data could work to alleviate macabre headlines by saving lives.

An Example of Effectual Usage

A famous mid-sized business owner found $400,000 by using Data Analytics. It seems that he had lost track 1,000 items of inventory, which was impeding his much desired cash-flow. The first day that he started his inventory, he saw the product that had not moved from the shelves.

He initiated a huge warehouse sale and sold the entire stock in one weekend, increasing his cash flow by $400,000. This more than paid for the implementation of the new database and peripherals. With the quick and decisive move to sell the new-found inventory, the company has utilized their data in a positive fashion with immediate results.

Previously this company had no IT department and did not have a POS system that traced product aging. He had money molding on the shelves. Once he had the database system installed, he was able to reduce older inventory by 40%, in addition to changing price points that were overblown, supplier costs, and profit margins. He also cleaned up the customer base with updated information, saving a substantial sum on postage and printing costs. With his new information, he can target the purchasers of the product to upgrade their sales rather than broadcasting mail to uninterested households. This company also uses their data to offer special discounts to their loyal and top customers, which generates income through upselling.

Chapter 5   The Different Types of Data Analytics

Big data is such a buzzword there is a misconception of what it is and what it does. The uses of Big Data are tremendous: fraud detection, competitive analysis, consumer preference analysis, traffic management, call center optimization, managing utility power grids, and managing warehouse and inventory, just to name only a few. Big data itself is problematic because it is the business intelligence code word for data overload.

There are three V's of Big data:

1. Too much data, or **volume**
2. Too much speed; the data is moving so quickly it cannot be analyzed, or **velocity**
3. Too much information from too many sources, or **variety**.

Even though the collection and assimilation of big data is daunting, the business intelligence that is derived from big data can aid a business immensely.

Four Kinds of Big Data Business Intelligence

There are four kinds of big data business intelligence that are particularly helpful for business owners:

1.   Prescriptive

2.   Predictive

3.   Diagnostic

4.   Descriptive

Prescriptive Analysis

Prescriptive analysis is the most valuable analysis because it informs the business what steps should be taken to improve the situation. The use of this data can be the beginning of change for the organization. Even though it is considered the most valuable, it is the least used as barely 3 percent of the organizations reported to use big data. Companies could use prescriptive analysis to give specific issues to isolated problems, such as in the health care industry and the problem of diabetes and obesity. Big data could identify the obese patients with both diabetes and high cholesterol, three contributing factors in the development of heart disease. These patients could be targeted immediately to initiate a four-fold attack on the risk factors through diet, diabetes education, exercise encouragement and cholesterol monitoring.

At present, the issues are addressed by different specialists, if they are even addressed at all. Combining treatment strategies would be much more effective and the combination of information could be compiled through prescriptive analysis.

Predictive Analysis

Predictive analysis is the prediction of possible scenarios derived from the analysis of the information. This is usually in the form of a business forecast. This form of analysis looks at the past to foretell the future. For example, the business might look at the previous Christmas sales to predict the future Christmas potential sales for a particular product. Predictive analysis is especially useful in marketing and sales departments to mimic previous campaigns that were successful. Some businesses are using predictive analysis to examine the sales process, from customer introduction, communications with the customer, the lead to the customer, the sale to the customer, the closing of the sale, and the follow-up communications.

Diagnostic Analytics

Diagnostic analysis focuses on past predicaments to discern the who, what and why of a situation. This analysis can use an analytic dashboard, or widgets that help the reader see at a glance the information at hand. An example of use of diagnostic analytics could be examining a sales campaign or a social media marketing campaign. With the widgets, one could see the number of posts, the number of visitors, the quantity of comments and likes, the page views and the feedback from the customer. Seeing these analytics at a glance instead of paging through reports brings a faster grasp of the salient points of the data. Utilizing diagnostic analytics will explain the failure of a marketing campaign to increase sales of a specific product.

Descriptive Analytics

This type of analytics gives real-time data on the current situation. Instead of giving last week's or even yesterday's data, this information is happening now. An example of the usage of descriptive analytics is pulling the current credit report for a customer desiring to purchase a new car. Examining the past behavior to assess the current credit risk and predict the future credit profile would help the sales manager determine if the potential customer can or will fulfill the credit contract.

Big data analytics will bring certain value to a company for the ROI because it fills in the blanks regarding customer performance and product sales. By reducing the enormity of big data into manageable chunks of information, a business owner can make better business decisions regarding staffing, sales, profits, and product variances.

Chapter 6   They all Work Together: Data Management, Data Mining, Data Integration and Data Warehousing

The terms for Big Data are many; this section of the book identifies the most useful terminology when addressing the logistics of big data.

Data management. Data management is the process of placing restrictions on the access and quality of data that flows in and through and out of an organization. Restrictions may include limited access, security measures to prevent viruses and corrupted data, and maintenance issues.

Data mining. Data mining is the process of sifting through the data to extract patterns and relevant information to solve the current issues in the business. Using software, data mining will take all the chaos out of the voluminous data.

Hadoop. This is open source software (meaning it's free!) to store data and run discriminating applications on commodity hardware. It is key to sifting the multiples of data information that is bombarding the data sets. It is known for the speed for which it processes data.

In-memory analytics. By investigating information from framework memory (rather than from your hard plate drive), you can get prompt bits of knowledge from your information and follow up on them rapidly. This innovation can expel information prep and investigative handling latencies to test new situations and make models; it's not just a simple route for businesses to stay agile and settle on better business choices, it likewise empowers them to run iterative and intelligent examination situations.

Predictive analytics. Predictive analytics uses, statistical algorithms, machine-learning techniques and data to identify the predictive outcomes based on previous patterns of usage. It's about giving a best evaluation on what will happen later, so businesses can feel more assured that they're settling on the best business choice. The most common and basic utilizations of predictive analytics incorporate misrepresentation and fraud, risk management, operations management and marketing functions.

Text mining. In utilizing text mining technology, the business you examine text data from the world wide web, comments, articles and other text sources to uncover insights that were previously unseen. Text mining incorporates machine learning and language processing to evaluate and sort web documents like blogs, feeds, intelligence on competitors, emails, comments and surveys to assist the business in analyzing quantities of information and discover tangents and hidden relationships.

Data integration is the combination of adding new information and data to an old computer system while keeping the data both clean and uncorrupted in content. Moving data effectively has become a challenge for businesses in the following areas:

- **Data Needs**

   - Delivering the correct data in the required format to alleviate the business needs is the primary reason for the integration of data. Every new source of data can impact the previous collection of information and systems to which it migrates.

- **Anticipating the Needs of the Business**
  - ○ Data is not helpful if it is not available in a timely fashion. Integration must be adequate to manage both batches of information and real-time

- **Confirm all Data is Stamped with Pertinent Information**

  - ○ Old systems did not time stamp or date activity in the server. For quick identification of the changes made to the data, the data integration needs to record this information.

- **Be Suspicious of All Incoming Data**

- It is natural to anticipate data from other sources, but be suspicious that it may be infected or other corrupt. Scan everything that comes in for compatibility and integration needs.

- **Validate Customer Information**

  - Compare incoming data to the master database to confirm the customer database is correct and current.

- **Keep a History of Every Change**

  - There is always a need to backtrack changes sometimes for statutory compliance and often when integration doesn't work as anticipated.

- **Upgrade the Systems and Evaluate the Process**

  - Constantly look for ways the system may be deficient for your business needs. Upgrade the systems regularly to ensure you have the best possible solution to your data management and integration needs.

Data Warehousing. Data warehousing is the storage of electronic data by the organization for which it is prepared. Data must be stored so that it is reliable, uncompromised, secure, easily retrievable and easily managed.

Chapter 7   Conducting Data Analysis for Your Business

We have stressed throughout this book the need for data analysis in the business enterprises, but we have yet to explain exactly how to collect data. This chapter will focus on basic data collection so that you can implement a strategy that will further your organizational goals.

A Step by Step Guide

What is Collecting Data?

Basically, gathering collected data implies putting your configuration for gathering data into operation. You've chosen how you're going to get data – whether by direct perception, interviews, overviews, investigations and testing, or different techniques – and now you and/or different spectators need to actualize your arrangement. There's more to gathering information, be that as it may. You'll need to record the information in suitable ways and sort the data so it's ideally helpful.

The way you gather your information ought to identify with how you're wanting to dissect and utilize it. Despite what strategy you choose to utilize, recording ought to be done simultaneous with information accumulation if conceivable, or soon thereafter, so nothing gets lost and memory doesn't blur.

Some of the functions necessary for useful data collection:

Assembling data from all sources.

Computing any numerical or comparative operations expected to get quantitative data prepared for examination. These might, for example, incorporate entering numerical perceptions into a diagram, table, or spreadsheet, or figuring the mean (normal), middle (midpoint), and/or mode (most every now and again happening) of an arrangement of numbers.

Coding information (deciphering information, especially subjective information that isn't communicated in numbers, into a structure that permits it to be handled by a particular programming project).

Arranging data in ways that make them simpler to work with.

How you do this will rely on upon your design of research and your assessment questions. You may amass perceptions by the independent variable (pointer of achievement) they identify with, by people or gatherings of members, by time, by movement, and so on. You may likewise need to group the collected information in a few distinctive ways, so you can consider interactions and relationships among various variables.

There are two sorts of variables in data. An independent variable (the intercession) is a condition executed by the analyst or group to check whether it will make change and improve the situation. This could be a project, strategy, framework, or other activity. A dependent variable is the situation that may change as a consequence of the independent variable or intercession. A dependent variable could be a conduct or a result.

How Do We Examine Data?

Investigating data includes looking at it in ways that reveal the connections, designs, patterns, and so on that can be found inside. That may mean subjecting it to statistical operations that can let you know not just what sorts of connections appear to exist among variables and additionally to what level you can believe the answers you're getting. It might mean contrasting your data with that from different data sets (a control group, statewide figures, and so on), to reach a few inferences from the information. The point, as far as your assessment, is to get a precise evaluation so as to better comprehend your work and its consequences.

There are two sorts of information you will use, even though not all assessments will fundamentally incorporate both. Quantitative data alludes to the data that is gathered as, or can be interpreted into, numbers, which can then be shown and broke down mathematically. Qualitative data are gathered as descriptions, accounts, conclusions, quotes, understandings, and so forth., and are by and large either not ready to be reduced to numbers, or are viewed as more important or enlightening if left as narratives. As you may anticipate, quantitative and qualitative data should be analyzed in different ways.

Quantitative data

Quantitative data is collected as numbers. Examples of quantitative data include:

- Frequency (rate and duration) of specific behaviors or situations
- Survey results (reported behaviors, ratings of customer satisfaction, etc.)
- Percentages of people with certain characteristics in the demographic (those with diabetes, obese, with heart disease indicators, the education level, etc.)

Data can also be collected other than numerically, and converted into quantitative data that is ready for analysis. Compilers can assign numbers to the levels of emphasis of a specific behavior. For instance, compilers can enumerate the quantity of Facebook "likes" or "comments". Whether or not this kind of information is necessary or helpful is dependent upon the kinds of questions your data is meant to answer.

Quantitative data is converted to statistical procedures such as calculating the mean number of times an event repeats. These calculations, because numbers are exacting, can offer definitive answers to varying questions. Quantitative analysis can identify changes in dependent variables that are related to – duration, frequency, timing intensity, etc. This allows comparative analysis with like issues, like changes within the population count of a zip code, or purchasing changes between women of a similar age.

Qualitative Data

Unlike numbers, qualitative information is considered "soft" data, meaning it can't be reduced to a specific conclusion. A number may indicate the population in a demographic, but the soft data may tell you the stress levels of the shoppers by the attitude and appearance of the customers.

Qualitative data can occasionally be converted into numbers, by counting the number of times specific things happen, or by assigning numbers to levels of importance, customer satisfaction or whether a function is user friendly when placing an order on a website.

The translation of qualitative data into quantitative data is dependent upon the human factor. Even if the customers agree to use the numbers 1-5 (1 being very unsatisfied and 5 being extremely satisfied) to evaluate customer satisfaction, there is still the issue of where 2, 3, and 4 fall on the assessment scale. The numbers only give a partial assessment; they give no information about the "why" of the customer rating.

Was the customer unhappy because of the product inventory on the shelf, a detail about the product, a problem with the atmosphere or music in the store, the location of the store, etc.?

Likewise, when counting specific instances of a behavior, did the counter include those who exhibited only partial behaviors (those that hit "like" but did not comment on Facebook, for example)?

Qualitative data can impart particular knowledge that is not available in quantitative data, such as why a sales campaign is working, or how the campaign is culturally conflicting with the customer base. (In 1962, Chevrolet was puzzled why their new "Nova" was so popular in the United States but had almost no sales in Mexico. Researchers failed to translate the word "Nova" into Spanish, which means "no go." The Spanish vernacular for the name of the car was "doesn't run." No wonder sales were down in Mexico! The automobile was renamed to Caribe and sales increased.)

It is often helpful to evaluate both quantitative and qualitative data sets.

What are the steps to collecting and analyzing data?

- Clearly design and define the measurements that are required to answer the questions.

- Conduct the research for the needed period of time in the correct timeframe.

- Organize the data dependent on the function of the data; how will you use the information?

- If possible and appropriate, change qualitative data into quantitative data.

-

- Use graphs and visualization charts (examples are in Chapter 10) to make the data easier to assimilate.

- Visually inspect the patterns of information to identify trends and connections.

- Seek patterns in the qualitative data, just like the quantitative data. If people consistently refer to similar problems, these may be crucial to understanding the problem and a workable solution.

Interpret the findings by using one of the following categories:

- Your marketing plan is performing on target with no obvious problems.

- Your marketing plan had no significant effect on sales.

- Your marketing plan had a negative effect on sales. (Possibly it was offensive or deemed silly by consumers.)

- Your marketing plan had mixed results. The promoted product sold well but a previously popular product may have decreased sales. For example, Secret deodorant offered a new scent category that was very popular but the unscented product sales decreased significantly as loyal users just swapped their preferences.

- If the analysis shows your marketing program is working you have a simple choice of continuing the program or tweaking it to hopefully increase sales.

- If analysis shows the program isn't working, interpretation is more convoluted. What is missing from the equation? What factor is preventing the desired results?

Analyzing and interpreting the results brings you full circle in the process; now you can use the knowledge you've gain to adjust your business and improve your service. Continuing to analyze and evaluate the business goals and results will keep the business current and an effective presence in the marketplace.

Chapter 8   An Organizational Approach to Data Analytics

This chapter discusses the framework that needs to be in place in the organization that incorporates big data into the corporate culture. A workable analytics governance will enable the business to utilize big data for an edge over the competition.

The Framework

To integrate information technology, business intelligence, and analytics four dominant questions must be under consideration:

1. Are analytics a key component of the business, in the same categories as finance, sales, product development, research and marketing?

2. Are the appropriate personnel in place?

3. Do the personnel have the ability for deep knowledge of the business needs?

4. Is there a governance structure in place?

This framework is referred to as the CSPG framework.

- Culture

- o Does the business revolve around the data analytics or does analytics take a backseat to marketing, R&D, and sales?

- Staffing

  - o Is there adequate staffing and is hiring of qualified staff a priority? Does the IT department work on a shoestring budget or do they have the proper resources to conduct big data analysis?

- Processes

  - o If the analytics process is completed correctly, data can be traded with like organizations without fear of contamination, allowing multiple streams of information.

- Governance

    o Governance is a new concept for businesses that have come recently to the table of data analytics. The governance needs a structure that encompasses people, structure, and salaries so that the IT department is not out of variance with the other departments.

Placement of the Analytics Function in the Business

There are three models for placement of the Data Analytics function:

1. Placing the analytics department in a central unit. The advantage of this location is that it is

easy to obtain data, integration into the company culture is simpler, and the data retrieval is faster. The challenge for a centralized department can be the location (as an add-on department it may be located away from the hub of decision makers), there may be confusion as to whom the department reports, and the data analysts may be so far away from the corporate culture that they cannot anticipate the business needs.

The second possibility is to decentralize the analytics and place analysts in each department throughout the company. This allows the analysts to focus on the business sector in which they reside. The challenge is to work together on company-wide projects that are not segmented and need all the analysts focused on one problem set.

2. The third option is a mix of the two previous scenarios. This places the analysts in a centralized location but also deploys analysts throughout the organization. This requires a very large staff of analysts, which may be the biggest challenge for the business.

The Key Analytics

Analytics is composed of models, infrastructure and operations. The models are statistical or predictive or datamining that are originated from statistical data. Key to the analytics process is the building of the models, which is usually performed by the analysts or data scientists or statisticians.

Infrastructure is the software components, applications used and platforms utilized for data management, data processing and decision making. The processes connected to analytics infrastructure are data management, model deployment and multiple analytics that must be incorporated in the business operations.

Operation are the processes that create the data used for models and actions for business use. Data can be purchased, internal, external, or collaborative.

The Data Analytics team must identify the internal and external relevant data, manage the data, build the analytical models and introduce the models into the internal systems. Most businesses organize these functions thusly: The business department requests the model, the Analytics team constructs the model, the IT department supplies the raw data, and operations launches the model. This brings us to the why of analytics governance.

Analytics Governance

The three challenges that businesses face when extracting big data are:

1. Identifying the unique needs for which the data will be used

2. Obtaining the needed information

3. Deploying the analytics models into the organization

The analytics manager must have enough authority to negate these challenges. The structure of governance needs a mechanism for identification, communications and resolution of issues stemming from data analysis problems. The analytics manager also needs the flexibility to hire qualified and knowledgeable personnel.

Chapter 9   Data Visualization

Visualization is what makes data come alive to the reader. A list of information can be a struggle to try to translate into useable data; translating the groups of data into a manageable form is essential to help the reader differentiate between the important and the superfluous.

Using graphic designing software can draw notice to the key statistics, and by using visual images, can uncover hidden patterns and connections that might not otherwise be detected.

The following is a list of _**free**_ data visualization software programs that are easily accessible on the web:

Chart.js

http://www.chartjs.org/

This program offers 6 different graphics HTML5, and is one of the most popular small-charting programs.

Dygraphs

dygraphs.com/

This is a JavaScript charting tool that is customizable, works with almost all browsers, and is used for dense data sets. It is mobile device and tablet friendly.

FusionCharts

www.fusioncharts.com/

FusionCharts Suite XT offers more than 90 charts, 965 data maps, and customizable, interactive business dashboard. FusionCharts is AJAX application-friendly and can be used with JavaScript API.

Instant Atlas

www.instantatlas.com/

Instant Atlas combines statistics with map data, which is very useful with demographic information.

Raw

raw.densitydesign.org/

Raw is customizable and available for modification, can be uploaded from the app to the compute, exported as SVG or PNG, can be embedded into the webpage, and offers vector-based images.

Tableau

www.tableau.com/

Tableau allows the user to drag and drop data to
update immediately into real-time charts.

Timeline

https://timeline.knightlab.com/

Timeline gives a detailed analysis of events that offers
a clickable ability to open the chart for more
particularized information.

Visual.ly

visual.ly/

Visual.ly is a gallery tool and an infographic tool. With
Visual.ly one can build stunning representations of
data that are brilliant and easy to create.

Visualize Free

https://visualizefree.com/

Visualize Free allows you to upload your own data sets and build HTML5 interactive charts for visualization.

ZingChart

https://www.zingchart.com/

ZingChart is another JavaScript charting program that has interactive Flash and HTML5 charts, more than 100 selections for your data analysis.

Chapter 10 Using Social Media

Domo released the infographic of statistics for Social Media users in 2015. Here are the statistics showing the phenomenal increase in users.

In just one minute,

BuzzFeed streams 34,000+ videos

Instagram displays 1.7 million+ photos

Netflix streams 80,000 video hours

Vine streams 1,000,000 videos

YouTube has uploads of 300 hours of video

Facebook has more than 4.1 million likes for posts (this is not the same as posts quantity as everyone does not take the time to like)

Twitter has 347,000 tweets

Obviously Social Media is now a major player for reaching consumers. A successful implementation of integration with social media and business practices can only enhance the opportunities for customer development. It would be wise for businesses to search for their products to find the answers to their tricky troubleshooting problems.

One of the often-neglected sources of information for a retail-related business is YouTube videos. Customers often make available videos that demonstrate how-to's that are not available in the product user manual. Sometimes Frequently Asked Questions writers are stymied at a little-known product failure. YouTube may have the answer that can be a solution if the Analysts engage in data mining.

Social Media Analytics

Social media analytics is using gathered information from blogs and social media websites to make a business more successful and more visible. Having an Internet presence is key to attracting younger generations of customers. Eighty-one percent of purchasers under 30 use the Internet to influence their purchases. A connection point to these purchasers is primary to business growth and development.

Social media analytics involves the practice of data mining, analysis of website information, data gathering, and utilizing the information for business forecasting and product shaping. The primary use of social media analytics is to evaluate customer responses to support marketing progress and customer service decisions. The second major use of social analytics is to get an edge over the competitor by maintaining a presence on the web. The third use for social media analysis is to gauge the customer sentiment regarding a product or service. The fourth use for social media analysis is to enhance the products by offering web only resources and discounts. The fifth use of social media analysis is for producing products that are contrary to logic (like runners pulling the lining out of running shoes because it makes their feet too hot) but desired by the consumer.

Social media analysis is similar to any other data analysis, but has specific needs to consider such as:

Form the hypothesis

Social media analysis is more about why something happened and less about reporting the event itself. Begin the analysis with of a circumstance or even with a question of why. Why did readers engage with this question but not respond to a similar survey on Facebook or Twitter? Examine the posting frequency and times you post. Are they optimal for your brand or product? For example, advertising for a food delivery would be much more effective at 5:00 than at 2:00 in the afternoon, as customers are hungry and tired when they leave work and want an instant solution to the dinner-hour dilemma.

Utilize the information to identify new ways of sharing information that attracts increased reader traffic. For example, Twitter now allows Vine videos to be embedded into posts. A hypothesis for testing would be: Does the new addition to Twitter increase traffic to the website or just entertain the readers more fully?

Move the Data to a Spreadsheet

Start with identifying trends and patterns on the spreadsheet. From this data you can extrapolate issues and variances for exploration.

Expand the Sample to Encompass as Much Data as you Possibly Can

Expanding the sample can be accomplished in many ways, but here are two of the possibilities: changing the end date of the sample, or tracking the competitors also.

Question the Results

It is easy to determine a false correlation when there is more data than one needs. Just like proof-testing, it can be a quick resolution by finding data to support your anticipated and desired outcome. Continue to test the results to eliminate bias in the conclusions.

Tools to Help Manage Social Media

Posting to several social media outlets day by day is time consuming, but also necessary. Rather than devote several hours a day to maintaining social media updates, consider some of the following tools that take the drudge out of daily monitoring.

Here is a list of recommended tools to help the business owner complete the task in less time. Some of these tools are free, but most require a paid subscription.

Buffer, HootSuite, and Sprout Social

These tools allow you to log in one time and schedule the posts for the major social media outlets. You can perform more than one function at the same time, writing and scheduling a week's worth of posts, analyzing the efficacy, and sharing information.

SumAll, Social Express, Socialight

These programs send the data to you instead of you having to go to them for retrieval. You get to choose what reports interest you for your business.

Social Count, SharedCount, BuzzSumo

This program tracks your "shares" from the different URLs. You enter the URL and it spits out the "shares" per day, week and month. This saves time so that you don't surf from Website to Website seeking the information.

Social Media Strategies for the Business Owner

These are the most helpful tips for the small and medium business owner that is managing the business and the social media.

Use a business dashboard to consolidate your social media.

Complete all social media posts at the same time and schedule them ahead of time.

Watch the engagement of your posts.

Segment your audience for faster analysis.

Social media is here to stay and gets bigger and more complex every day. Managing social media is now essential to maintain a presence on the web. Businesses that are ignoring social media with their heads hidden in the sand like ostriches are losing the opportunity for a new income stream. Online sales of products are increasing more every moment. In one minute, Amazon has over 4,000 new customers purchase a product. A savvy business owner will want to tap that potential customer base as quickly as possible.

Social media analytics helps the business owner target customers that are already interested in the product or service promoted by the organization. With a little attention to the customer service needs of the consumer, a pathway may be discovered that opens the gateway for communication and sales through the Internet outlet.

Chapter 11 How Data Analytics Can Sustain any Business

The Age of Analytics has dawned and the Age of Aquarius has moved on. Organizations that collect, interpret, and act on the raw data they derive can change to the rapidly moving marketplace, and stay well ahead of the competition.

To use the data correctly and quickly, analyzing the data with these tools will bring clarity and innovative suggestions.

Begin with **Measuring**, determines which analytics will be most helpful for decision making within the firm.

Diagnose the problems that have occurred with customer satisfaction or product placement. Why has something happened in an adverse way? Data analytics can help you locate the specific issue for a satisfying solution.

Predict and Optimize to forecast changes and the potential consequences of the change. Use the "if"..."then" method of questioning. (If I make this change with customer service how can I then anticipate the reaction?) This analytical technique helps to determine the direction of the organization and the best route to sustain continued growth.

Operationalize, or placing the information into use by the front-line workers, sales staff, engineers, marketers, managers and the remaining decision makers. This is the transition from analysis to usefulness, leaving the laboratory and moving into real-world experience.

Automation is when the business managers use real-time information to make immediate changes in the organization. For example, in a grocery industry, couponing is a big money maker for both the customer and the grocer. The grocer moves the product but is reimbursed by the couponing agency, along with a processing fee based on the value of the coupon. The customer receives the product at a reduced price, and the product is usually a newly introduced item that would be considered a luxury item in a depressed economy. What happens, though, when the customer takes advantage of the retailer by purchasing all of the shelf stock of the product, leaving none for the following customers and creating an environment of disgruntled customers? The store manager immediately assesses the situation and applies a "3 coupons only per transaction" rule. Now the customer can still purchase the item but very few want to leave the checkout to make more than one transaction. The retail grocer has used automation to analyze the problem and create an immediate solution.

The last stage of implementation is **transformation**, when the business moves to a data-driven corporate culture, making business decisions based on current analytics instead of tradition or gut instinct.

How You Can Collect Data for Analysis Today

1.   Establish a digital presence that both gives and receives information. Before you can collect data you need a way like a social media outlet and an interactive website.

2.   Remember your goal is to receive, sort, and address the data you have collected from as many sources as possible, as quickly as possible so the data won't be stale or even unreliable. The more data you collect the more accurate your findings will be.

3.   Focus on the questions that need answers. It will be tempting to read and ponder everything, but that will defeat the purpose of collecting the data. Keeping the questions at the forefront of your mind will help you mine the customer intelligence for the necessary information to change your business practices into a positive spin.

4.   Engage with your customers through social media. Don't assume you know what they want. Give them plenty of opportunities to push the like button. This valuable button will target the customers' wants and needs much better than a formal questionnaire.

5.   Use Google Analytics and Alex to determine relevant information regarding your client base. They have easy-to-understand statistics on website traffic and SEO rankings. Use this information to cater to your clientele. Just changing a few keywords on your site can increase your traffic and move you to number one in the Google search engine, a prime place for attracting new customers and readers.

Conclusion

Thank you again for downloading this book, ***Data Analytics: Practical Data Analysis and Statistical Guide to Transform and Evolve Any Business, Leveraging the power of Data Analytics, Data Science, and Predictive Analytics for Beginners***!

I hope this book was able to help you to understand and utilize data analytics to increase your business sales, marketing and efficiency.

The next step is to implement the policies and procedures that are presented in this guide to data analytics.

Finally, if you enjoyed this book, please take the time to share your thoughts and post a review on Amazon. It'd be greatly appreciated!

Thank you and good luck!

Please Checkout my Other titles in the " Hacking Freedom and Data Driven" series

Hacking University: Freshman Edition
Essential Beginner's Guide on How to Become
an Amateur Hacker (Hacking, How to Hack,
Hacking for Beginners, Computer Hacking)

HACKING
UNIVERSITY
FRESHMAN EDITION
Essential Beginner's Guide on How to Become an Amateur Hacker
(Hacking, How to Hack, Hacking for Beginners, Computer Hacking)

ISAAC D. CODY

"This book provides basic information and breaks down all the terminology into easy-to-understand descriptions. It also goes over the history (which was fun to read) as well as all the different types of hacking. The screen shots were very helpful as well. It concludes directions on how to gain more knowledge and mastery in security/hacking. Helpful beginner guide for sure!" – Rachael T.

Made in the USA
San Bernardino, CA
30 November 2016